Chicago

A PHOTOGRAPHIC PORTRAIT II

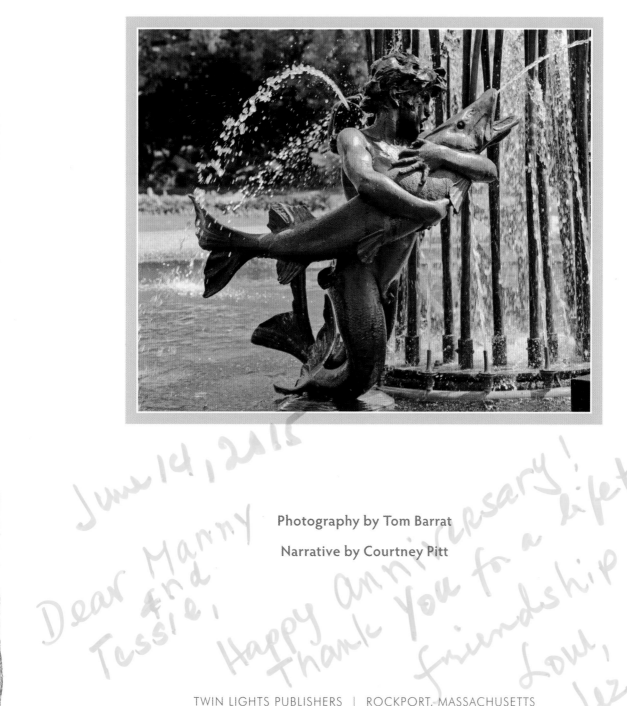

Photography by Tom Barrat

Narrative by Courtney Pitt

June 14, 2015

Dear Manny and Tessie,

Happy Anniversary! Thank you for a lifetime of friendship.

Love,
Jez & Edna

TWIN LIGHTS PUBLISHERS | ROCKPORT, MASSACHUSETTS

Copyright © 2013 by
Twin Lights Publishers, Inc.

All rights reserved. No part of this book may
be reproduced in any form without written
permission of the copyright owners. All images
in this book have been reproduced with the
knowledge and prior consent of the artists
concerned and no responsibility is accepted
by producer, publisher, or printer for any
infringement of copyright or otherwise, arising
from the contents of this publication. Every effort
has been made to ensure that credits accurately
comply with information supplied.

First published in the United States of America by:

Twin Lights Publishers, Inc.
51 Broadway
Rockport, Massachusetts 01966
Telephone: (978) 546-7398
http://www.twinlightspub.com

ISBN: 978-1-934907-18-4

10 9 8 7 6 5 4 3 2

(*opposite*)
Fountain of Time

(*frontispiece*)
Bates Fountain

(*jacket front*)
Cloud Gate

Book design by:
SYP Design & Production, Inc.
www.sypdesign.com

Printed in China

Chicago is rich in history. Long before the first permanent resident arrived in Chicago, the area was inhabited by various Native American tribes including the Potawatomi. Surviving primarily on trade and seasonal hunting, they named this area "Chicagoua," after the wild garlic that grew on its riverbanks.

It wasn't until 1671, when Native American guides revealed Chicago's portage to French explorers Louis Joliet and Father Marquette, that it was realized how strategically valuable Chicago's location was for commerce. With the Chicago River linking the Great Lakes to the Mississippi River system, a key route was created across the continent expanding trade and exploration of the Mississippi Valley and beyond.

When settlers began to move westward, the United States Army built Fort Dearborn in 1803 and with it came many soldiers and their families. During the War of 1812, hostilities flared between Native Americans and the soldiers, which resulted in the fort being burned to the ground. One year later, Fort Dearborn was rebuilt and settlers returned. Today, the outlined corners of the fort can be seen on Michigan Avenue and Wacker Drive.

It wasn't long before Chicago became a hub for commerce and industry. With the building of the city's first railroad in 1848 as well as the opening of the Illinois and Michigan Canal, moveable bridges were soon installed to aid large ships traveling down the river.

After the election of Abraham Lincoln and the Civil War, the city underwent rapid population growth and expansion. In 1871, the Great Chicago Fire decimated most of the city and out of its ashes and rubble arose a new, more modern city. The World's Columbian Exposition in 1893 produced museum collections, cultural buildings, and rebuilt the city with a plan from Daniel Burnham. Chicago steamed forward and hasn't looked back. Skyscrapers, monuments, sculptures, and art heralded in the 20th century along with big personalities and big ideas.

Chicago: A Photographic Portrait introduces you to this grand city of the new millennium through stunning photographs by Tom Barrat. Capturing "The Windy City" with an insider's view and a kaleidoscope of images, it is easy to see why Chicago attracts both visitors and locals alike.

Chicago River

With 38 movable bridges along the North Branch, South Branch, and Main Stem, a boat tour along the Chicago River is one of the best ways to see Chicago's world-renowned architecture. This view is from the Main Stem looking west toward the Trump International Hotel and Tower.

Chicago Board of Trade (opposite)

Sitting as a capstone in the LaSalle Street canyon, the Art Deco style limestone building designed by architects Holabird & Root has been home to commodities trading since 1930. The Roman goddess Ceres rests atop the building holding a bag of corn in one hand and a sheaf of wheat in the other.

BP Pedestrian Bridge (above)

Snaking over Columbus Drive from Millennium Park to Grant Park, the BP Bridge, with flat interlocking steel shingles and Brazilian hardwood floor boards, is a functional piece of art. Designed by Frank Gehry and opened in 2004, the bridge offers exceptional views of Lake Michigan.

Centennial Fountain

Part of the Centennial Plaza, a water arc shoots across the Chicago River at the top of every hour from morning to night in the summer. Some boaters take advantage of its cool mist while others stop to enjoy the show.

Centennial Plaza and Fountain *(top and bottom)*

In 1989 the Chicago Dock and Canal Trust donated land on the north side of the Chicago River to commemorate the centennial of the Metropolitan Water Reclamation District of Greater Chicago. Water cascades over the polished red granite, concrete, and limestone fountain from Memorial Day to Labor Day.

9

Chicago Riverwalk *(above and opposite)*

Known as Chicago's "second shoreline" and stretching from Lake Shore Drive to Franklin Street, the Riverwalk is full of professionals enjoying a minute outside of the office and is a hub of activity on weekends. Celebrated restaurants, bike rentals, architectural tours, water taxis, and much more create a vibrant atmosphere.

Bates Fountain (above)

As a centerpiece of the Formal Garden in Lincoln Park, this bronze and granite fountain was donated in 1887 by Eli Bates. Also known as "Storks at Play," even though most experts agree the birds are geese, Augustus Saint-Gaudens and Frederick MacMonnies' creation was fully restored in 1999.

Magdalene (opposite)

Inspired by Greek mythology, sculptor Dessa Kirk created four Daphne statues from recycled Cadillacs. The figures were so well received at the temporary exhibit from which they were commissioned that they were installed as permanent fixtures around the city in 2008. This single Daphne is located in Grant Park.

Daphne Garden (pages 14 -15)

Three Daphne sculptures, located on Northerly Island, look to the sky and appear to be taking flight. With leaves for arms and vines for hair, these graceful figures rest amongst native prairie grass and dramatic views of the city.

Monument to the Great Northern Migration

Bronzeville, known for famous residents Louis Armstrong and Muddy Waters, has been at the center of African-American culture since the 1920's. Alison Saar's sculpture embodies a north-facing man carrying a suitcase and a body covered in tattered soles, symbolizing the long journey of his people.

America's Courtyard

On the grounds of the Adler Planetarium, this spiral galaxy of granite and marble is the work of Denise Milan and Ary Perez and represents the harmonious link of South America and North America. The center stone is aligned with the compass directions of North, South, East, and West.

Buckingham Fountain

Built in 1927 and inspired by a fountain
at Versailles, this granite and pink Georgia
marble landmark in Grant Park is one
of the largest fountains in the world.
Designed by architect Edward H. Bennett
to symbolize Lake Michigan, the fountain
has a 20-minute water show every hour
in the summer.

Elks National Veterans Memorial

Free and open to the public, this monument and national headquarters is impressive both inside and out. Two reclining elk flank the stairs, while friezes and sculptures surround the facade. Inside, tributes to the armed services and Elk fraternal principles are illustrated in a breathtaking columned rotunda.

Man Enters the Cosmos

This 13-foot-tall sundial was created in
1980 by Henry Moore and is a modern
take on an ancient timekeeping device.
Located on the grounds outside the
planetarium, this magnificent sculpture was
commissioned in honor of the "Golden Years
of Astronomy," when space exploration
turned from a dream to a reality.

Adler Planetarium

Located on Museum Campus, America's first planetarium opened in 1930 and houses one of the finest collections of astronomical artifacts. With three theaters, extensive exhibits, and the world's leading space science center; the planetarium's focus is on inspiring young people to pursue science careers.

Rosenberg Fountain (opposite)

Wealthy businessman Joseph Rosenberg gifted to Chicago a drinking fountain, "to provide the thirsty with a drink." Installed in 1893, this miniature Greek temple is topped with the goddess Hebe, cupbearer of the gods. Cast in Munich by sculptor Franz Machtl, it is located in Grant Park.

Agora (above)

One hundred and six headless and armless figures appear to wander aimlessly through Grant Park. Created by Polish artist Magdalena Abakanowicz and installed in 2006, these 9-foot-tall controversial figures are made of rusted iron and are valued at about 3 million dollars.

Lincoln Park Conservatory *(top and bottom)*

All year round Chicagoans, brides, and tourists enjoy this magnificent tropical oasis. Inside the Victorian glass dome are four separate display houses; the Palm House, the Fernery, the Orchid House, and the Show House. An outdoor French garden is located adjacent to the historic Grandmother's Garden.

Lincoln Park

It is no wonder that this park, packed with everything from a nature museum, a lily pool, a theater on the lake, a zoo, as well as a golf course, basketball and tennis courts, a target archery field, and so much more, is the second most visited park in the United States. And, best of all, it's free!

Chicago Botanic Garden

For over 40 years, this living plant museum in Glencoe has been a garden oasis for both locals and visitors to relax, contemplate, and celebrate. The garden is situated on more than 385 acres with 2.5 million plants, 25 display gardens, and four natural growth areas.

Evening Island *(top)*

Each Monday evening in the summer, carillonneurs delight visitors to a 45-minute musical performance. A collection of bells that are played manually, this carillon bell tower, complete with 48 bronze bells forged in Holland, has been a landmark at the garden since 1986.

Carolus Linnaeus Statue *(bottom)*

Linnaeus, known as the father of environmental science, created a system in the 1700's to classify plants, animals, and minerals, which is still used today. In this bronze sculpture by Robert Berks, he is portrayed with his collection bag on his back and enthusiastically reaching for another exciting find.

Humboldt Park (top and bottom)

Internationally known for his landscape architecture, Jens Jensen created a flawless example of his Prairie-style landscape architecture on the northwest side of the city. The boathouse pavilion as well as the Humboldt Park Stables and Receptory, now the Puerto Rican Arts and Culture Museum, have been designated Chicago Landmarks.

Batcolumn (opposite)

As "an emblem to Chicago's ambition and vigor," this 100-foot-tall open latticework sculpture by Claes Oldenburg, was dedicated in 1977. Fascinated with depicting ordinary objects in colossal scale, this baseball bat caused a great deal of controversy; but now this two baseball team town adores this piece of art.

Chicago Evening (pages 30 -31)

With most of downtown Chicago destroyed by the Great Fire of 1871, Chicagoans quickly rebuilt the city which was laid out by leading architects. Today, it has world class hotels, shopping, restaurants, nightlife, and culture. International retailers, domestic firms, and local artisans all thrive in harmony to make Chicago unique.

Wrigley Building *(above)*

With its east and south facades brightly lit at night, the Wrigley Building's clock tower is easy to locate along the Chicago River. Built on the approximate site of Chicago's first home, the glazed terra-cotta structure is actually two towers connected by two sky-bridges and a ground floor walkway.

Chicago Water Tower *(opposite)*

This 154-foot-tall limestone, neo-Gothic structure sits in the heart of the Magnificent Mile and is a symbol of Chicago's resilience. As one of only two public structures in downtown Chicago to survive the Great Chicago Fire of 1871, it now houses the City Gallery with a rotation of Chicago themed photography.

Millennium Park

Railroad tracks, parking lots, and unused train cars are a distant memory for this civic collaboration. A triumph of public space, its highlights include the Jay Pritzker Pavilion, Crown Fountain, Cloud Gate, McCormick Tribune Ice Rink, and the Lurie Garden. The BP Bridge connects the park with Daley Bicentennial Plaza.

Art Institute of Chicago *(above and right)*

Housing over 260,000 works of art by such masters as Monet, Renoir, and Van Gogh; this museum's galleries are full of rare treasures for everyone, including the Touch Gallery for the visually impaired. Two beloved lion sculptures flank the entrance and are decorated for the holidays and sporting events.

Modern Wing (top)

With the opening of the Modern Wing in 2009, the Art Institute of Chicago became the second largest art museum in our nation. Housing the museums 20th- and 21st-century art, this new, light-filled expansion by Renzo Piano includes several public spaces that are free of charge to the public.

McCormick Tribune Ice Rink (bottom)

Operated by the Chicago Department of Cultural Affairs and built by the McCormick Tribune Foundation, this special ice rink in Millennium Park is open and free to the public during the winter months. In the summer months, it becomes an open air restaurant with special cultural and musical events.

Miró's Chicago (opposite)

A mixture of cubism, surrealism, and Catalan folk art, this work originally titled *The Sun, The Moon, and One Star* is by Joan Miró. The 40-foot-tall sculpture, located in Brunswick Plaza and across from the Picasso sculpture, was unveiled in 1981 and represents a woman with outstretched arms.

Fountain of the Great Lakes

Commissioned to create a sculpture that represented one of the Midwest's greatest resources, Illinois native Lorado Taft completed *Fountain of the Great Lakes* in 1913. Located on the grounds of the Art Institute, five female figures are arranged so that water flows from their shells the same way it flows through the Great Lakes.

Five Great Shells

Although some did not approve of these five scantily clad women (who were modeled after and created by five of Taft's female students), the unveiling of this magnificent sculpture was met with much fan-fare. Today, Taft is recognized for creating some of Chicago's best-known sculptures.

Union Stock Yard Gate *(above)*

This imposing, limestone gate is one of the few remaining structures from Chicago's once thriving livestock and meatpacking industry that earned Chicago the nickname, "Hog Butcher of the World." Built in 1875 and commissioned by Superintendent John B. Sherman, Sherman's prized bull is featured at the top of the gate.

Old Stock Exchange Entrance *(opposite)*

The Chicago Stock Exchange building was designed by Louis Sullivan and completed in 1894. With the efforts of the Landmarks Preservation Council, this arch was saved when the building was torn down in 1972. Today, it is located on the east side of the Art Institute and considered a masterpiece.

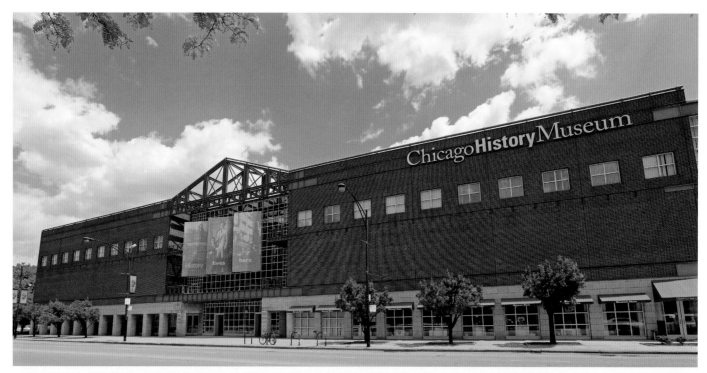

Chicago History Museum *(top)*

With over 22 million artifacts and documents, the Chicago History Museum provides an overview of the city's history as well as that of prominent Chicagoans. Founded as the Historical Society in 1856, it is nationally recognized for its exclusive treasures, which include Lincoln's death bed and Michael Jordan's uniform.

Chicago Children's Museum *(bottom)*

Located on historic Navy Pier, this museum is one of the largest children's museums in the country and includes three floors of interactive displays. Exhibits range from WaterWays and Treehouse Trails to the Kovler Family Climbing Schooner.

Chicago Public Library

The Chicago Public Library was established after the Great Chicago Fire from donations of over 8,000 books from Great Britain's "English Book Donation." Today, the Harold Washington Library Center, the central branch of the library, features a Talking Book Center, Children's Library, and Winter Garden with skylights.

Sue *(above and left)*

Visitors to the Museum are greeted by SUE, the largest and most complete Tyrannosaurus Rex ever discovered. Standing 13 feet tall, this 67-million-year-old dinosaur was discovered in 1990 in South Dakota and became the museum's esteemed relic in 2000 at a cost of over 8.3 million dollars.

Field Museum of Natural History

Founded to accommodate the biological and anthropological artifacts assembled for the World's Columbian Exposition of 1893, the museum houses more than 20 million specimens and 275,000 volumes of books and journals. Located on Museum Campus, it is considered one of the United States' preeminent natural history museums.

Museum of Science and Industry

Built for the 1893 World's Columbian Exposition, the Palace of Fine Arts building now houses the Museum of Science and Industry. Opened during the 1933 Century of Progress Exposition, it is the largest science museum in the Western Hemisphere featuring a U-505 German submarine and the *Apollo 8* spacecraft.

DuSable Museum of African American History *(top)*

The oldest and largest custodian of African American culture and art, this museum was named for Jean Baptiste Point du Sable, the first permanent, non-Native American settler in Chicago. The museum celebrates the achievements and contributions of African Americans.

Holocaust Museum & Education Center *(bottom)*

This museum and educational structure is the Midwest's main Holocaust memorial center. It opened in 2009 with special guest Elie Wiesel and keynote speaker Former President Bill Clinton. The centerpiece of the collection is a tattered German train boxcar as well as over 2,000 video testimonies of survivors.

Fountain of Time

More than 127 feet long and considered a masterpiece, sculptor Lorado Taft's "Time" symbolizes life's journey from birth to death. Commissioned to commemorate the 100 years of peace between the United States and Great Britain in the Treaty of Ghent, the sculpture of 100 flowing figures and reflecting pool was dedicated in 1922.

Shedd Aquarium *(top and bottom)*

Home to an impressive collection of underwater life, the Shedd Aquarium opened in 1930 and offers popular exhibits such as the Caribbean Reef, Amazon Rising, Wild Reef, and the world famous Abbott Oceanarium, where visitors find beluga whales, Pacific white-sided dolphins, sea otters, and sea lions.

Sitting on Museum Campus, the aquarium holds more than five million gallons of water with over 25,000 fish. The world's oldest captive fish, Granddad, an Australian lungfish, has been living at the aquarium since 1933.

Bahá'í House of Worship *(opposite)*

Located in Wilmette, this temple received its first cornerstone in 1903 and was dedicated in 1953. Constructed of delicately latticed concrete and quartz, visitors marvel at the beauty of this nine-sided building with its 138-foot-high dome, nine surrounding gardens, and nine reflecting pools.

Garfield Park Conservatory (above)

Conceived as a series of natural landscapes, Jens Jensen redesigned the conservatory in 1908 and today it is hailed as "landscape art under glass." This conservatory is one of the largest in the nation and features themed rooms all containing unique and rare plant species.

Bulls and Maidens (left)

Located on the grounds of the Garfield Park Conservatory are two sculptures entitled *Bulls with Maidens*. Created by sculptors Daniel French and Edward Potter for the World's Columbian Fair of 1893, smaller models were created in 1908 and made of bronze. This figure of a Native American goddess of corn symbolizes the "New World."

Garfield Park Fieldhouse

Known as the "Gold Domed Building" because of its gold-leaf covering, this Spanish Baroque revival style fieldhouse was built in 1928 as the West Park Commission Administration Building. Inside are beautiful features such as a colorful terrazzo floor, marble-clad walls with sculptured panels, and a dramatic two-story rotunda.

Peggy Notebaert Nature Museum
(above and left)

Built in 1999 as the new home for the Museum of the Chicago Academy of Sciences, the building designed by Perkins and Will is located in the heart of Lincoln Park. A leader in environmental conservation, the museum boasts the popular Butterfly Haven with warm-weather birds and more than 1,000 colorful butterflies.

Republic Statue *(opposite)*

Daniel French's small scale replica of the Republic Statue was completed in 1918 in celebration of the 25th anniversary of the 1893 World's Columbian Exposition and Illinois' 100th statehood anniversary. This gilded bronze statue stands 24 feet tall and is located in Jackson Park, the former location of the exposition.

Washington Park

When Fredrick Olmsted was hired in 1870 to create this 372-acre park, he laid out a field surrounded by trees and used grazing sheep to keep the grass short. Today, there is a thriving cricket and baseball program, and the old administrative building now houses the DuSable Museum.

Osaka Garden

Located in Jackson Park behind the Museum of Science and Industry, this one-of-a-kind Japanese garden was a gift from Japan for the 1893 World's Columbian Exposition to solidify American and Japanese relations. The bridge over the pond is the focal symbol connecting the two cultures.

Oriental Institute Museum Collection
(top and bottom)

As a pioneer in Near East studies, this institute was founded in 1919 by James Henry Breasted and is part of the University of Chicago. Highlights of the permanent museum collection include this 40-ton limestone lamassu (a winged bull with a human head) from Khorsabad and the head of a colossal bull made of dark gray limestone created between 486–424 BC.

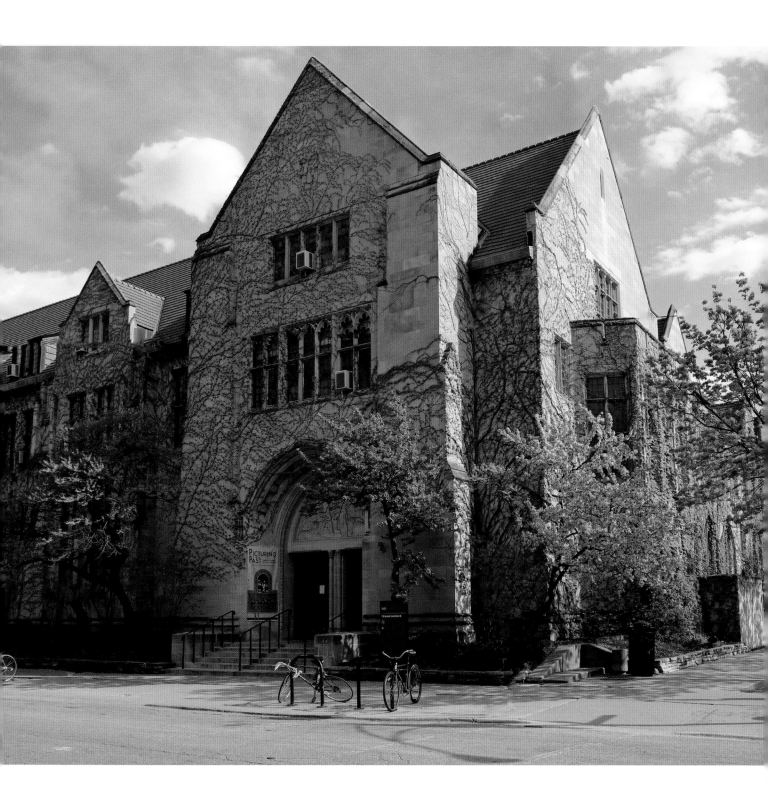

Oriental Institute Museum

Through the support of John D. Rockefeller, the institute moved to this building in 1931 and today is a renowned center for ancient Near East studies. Included in the collection are two "magic bricks" from an Egyptian tomb, a female mummy, a coffin for a lizard, and much more.

Sightseeing

An easy and fun way to view Chicago's architecture is by water. Many sightseeing companies operate on the river and offer visitors a choice of architecture tours, sunset tours, wine tasting tours, as well as combined river and lake excursions.

Water Taxi (top)

Wendella's yellow water taxis have been shuttling rush hour commuters up and down the Chicago River since 1962. During the summer months on the Main Branch, the taxis run in a loop from LaSalle Street to Michigan Avenue and on the South Branch from Madison to Chinatown.

St. Patrick's Day (bottom)

Beginning in 1962, the custom of dying the Chicago River green has become a favorite Chicago tradition. Both the Irish and the "Irish for the day" enjoy seeing the Chicago Journeymen Plumbers dye the river with a bio-responsible "Emerald Isle" shade of green.

Pritzker Pavilion *(above and opposite)*

Part of the Millennium Park's success is being open and accessible to the public, and this design by Frank Gehry is its centerpiece. With 4,000 fixed seats and 7,000 lawn seats on the Great Lawn under the stainless steel trellis, the Pavilion is considered a functional piece of art.

Cloud Gate *(pages 64 – 65)*

Selected as the winning designer from 30 potential candidates, Anish Kapoor's stainless steel artistic design has been nicknamed "The Bean" by Chicagoans. It sits in the middle of the AT&T Plaza as part of Millennium Park. The mirror-like surface reflects the skyline and clouds, hence the name Cloud Gate.

Four Seasons *(top and bottom)*

Marc Chagall's impressive understanding of color comes alive in this 1974 mosaic which depicts Chicago in the spring, summer, fall, and winter. The 14-foot-high, 70-foot-long rectangle is located on Dearborn and Monroe streets and was created in France, shipped in panels, and installed onsite.

Union Station

A Daniel Burnham design in the Beaux-Art style features a vaulted skylight, balconies, and grand staircases which have been featured in movies, as well as an open concourse along the river. The ornate Great Hall has been welcoming travelers from near and far since 1925.

Magnificent Mile (top)

Starting at the Chicago River and ending at Oak Street, the "Mag Mile" has some of the most luxurious hotels, restaurants, and retailers in the world – all on one avenue. It boasts many historic landmark designated buildings mingled harmoniously alongside some of the tallest and most fashionable buildings on the globe.

Hershey Building (bottom)

Located in Water Tower Park on Michigan Avenue, this chocolate mecca features one-of-a-kind confections and is a perfect stop for a sweet treat. Complete with a bake shop and singing baker, this is a favorite among locals and visitors alike.

Tulips on Michigan Avenue (opposite)

Every spring Chicago is transformed with blankets of bold colors along the Magnificent Mile when thousands of tulips come into bloom. Heralding in spring with the promise of warm weather and sunny skies ahead, Tulip Days take place from April to May and is one of the most breathtaking sights in the city.

Chicago Theater (opposite)

This magnificent 1921 movie house ushered in the grand era of motion pictures in an opulent style. With an interior modeled after Versailles and the Paris Opera House, the Tiffany stained glass and crystal chandeliers featuring Steuben glass shades still glitter today after a multimillion dollar renovation.

Marshall Field's Clock (top)

One of two "Great Clocks" installed on the Marshall Field's building, this one, located on the southwest side, was erected in 1897. Weighing more than 7 tons each, a Marshall Field's clock was featured in a Norman Rockwell drawing on a 1945 cover of the Saturday Evening Post.

Chicago Datum & Northern Trust (bottom)

In 1905, construction began on the corner of LaSalle and Monroe streets for The Northern Trust Bank. With a solid construction and concrete pillars reaching 105 feet below street level, city engineers later designated it the Number One City Datum Mark, the point from which future structures are measured vertically.

Flamingo

Alexander Calder's abstract sculpture, *Flamingo* is an example of the artists' playful humor. Resembling a whimsical bird, it is located amongst the boxy, glass buildings in Federal Plaza. A smaller version can be seen at the Modern Wing of the Art Institute.

Crown Fountain

An ingenious system of water, light, technology, and moving pictures create the two 50-foot-tall towers located in Millennium Park. Artist Jaume Plensa's sculpture fountains opened in 2004 to promote interaction with visitors through water, and features faces of local residents spouting water intermittently.

Chinatown *(top)*

With the completion of the transcontinental railroad, many Chinese migrated east from California and settled in Chicago. By 1905, Chicago's Chinatown was established and today is a tribute to Chinese culture. Modeled after a wall in Beijing, *Nine Golden Dragons* signifies the Chinese focus on good fortune.

Welcome Gate *(bottom)*

Completed in 1993, Chinatown welcomes visitors through its colorful, two-level gate. Known as a unique place to visit all year round for everything from concerts in Ping Tom Park, walking and food tours, to a terrific Chicago Marathon Rallying station; Chinatown is a thriving neighborhood and business district.

Pillar of Fire *(opposite)*

Resting atop the original spot where the Great Chicago Fire started on De Koven Street is a 33-foot-tall bronze sculpture of intertwined flames. In 1961, sculptor Egon Weiner, an instructor at the Art Institute, created the piece that sits at the entrance of the Chicago Fire Department Academy.

Monument with Standing Beast

Described by the artist as "a drawing which extends into space," this 29-foot-tall fiberglass sculpture was installed in front of the James R. Thompson Center in 1984. Known for his urban style of using graffiti, caricature, and street language, this was one of Jean Dubuffet's last works before he died.

National Museum of Mexican Art

Located in the Pilsen neighborhood, this is the largest Latino museum in the United States. Founded in 1982 by Carlos Tortolero along with fellow educators, it showcases the beauty and richness of Mexican culture. Permanent collections include folk art, textiles, photography, paintings, and sculptures.

John Hancock Center *(opposite)*

Designed by Skidmore, Owings and Merrill and completed in 1970, the 100-story John Hancock Center is an award winning example of structural expressionist architecture. With shops, luxury condominiums, office space, fine dining, a 44th-floor sky lobby pool, and 94th-floor observatory, it is an icon along Michigan Avenue.

94th Floor Observatory *(top)*

Visitors are treated to a 360 degree view of the city from the Observatory of the John Hancock Center. Take a Sky Tour or step out onto the Skywalk, an open-air viewing platform, and see why Chicago is nicknamed, "The Windy City."

Jackson Park *(bottom)*

The site of the 1893 World's Columbian Exposition, Jackson Park transformed from a swamp into an internationally revered crowning achievement. Many original buildings no longer exist, but the Museum of Science and Industry and the Japanese Garden still stand. The park is a splendid cornerstone of the South Side.

Willis Tower Skydeck (*above*)

Installed in 2009, retractable glass balconies extend approximately four feet over Wacker Drive and 1,353 feet up in the air. Stepping out onto The "Ledge" is an exhilarating way to view the city and feel the tower sway in the wind. On a clear day, visibility is approximately 40-50 miles.

Willis Tower (*opposite*)

Structural engineer Fazlur Khan and architects from Skidmore, Owings and Merrill were credited with the creation of the bundled tube system that was revolutionary in 1973 when the Sears Tower opened. Renamed the Willis Tower in 2009, the bundled tube style is fundamental to today's tall building designs.

Merchandise Mart (above)

Sitting upon a former Native American trading post, the "Mart," as it is known to Chicagoans, has been part warehouse, part department store, and part office building since 1930. Spanning almost two city blocks, with over 30 elevators and a 25 story center tower, the Mart is located along the north bank of the Chicago River.

Marina City (opposite)

Built in 1964, these twin corncob-shaped towers are the anchor for Marina City which includes the House of Blues, restaurants, a marina, a bowling alley, a hotel, and much more. At 65 stories, this city within a city stands out in contrast to the surrounding conventional buildings.

84

Chicago Cultural Center
(opposite, top and bottom)

Originally the Chicago Public Library in 1897, this opulent building is now home to the Chicago Cultural Center. The nation's first free municipal cultural center, it attracts thousands of visitors each year to its programs and exhibits as well as to view the world's largest Tiffany glass dome.

Crossing *(above)*

Hubertus von der Goltz's eye catching sculpture of a figure traversing a bridge on precarious footing was installed in 1998 along LaSalle Street. As a gateway between the Loop and River North, this 25-foot-tall sculpture symbolizes the delicate balance between thought, action, and existence.

Picasso Sculpture *(opposite)*

Standing 50 feet tall in Daley Plaza, the untitled Pablo Picasso sculpture was unveiled in 1967. Now a beloved symbol of the city, it is said that the sculpture was inspired by a French woman who posed for Picasso in 1954 wearing a high ponytail.

Pullman Historic District *(top)*

America's first planned industrial community, Pullman's factory town included a school, fire department, church, market square, and hotel. Homes were provided with running water, gas, and front and back yards. Today, the community focuses on preserving its heritage and many of the homes look as they did in the 1880's.

Frank Lloyd Wright *(bottom)*

Known as the father of Prairie-style architecture, Frank Lloyd Wright lived and worked in this house from 1889 -1909. Today, it is open to public tours, having been painstakingly refurbished to its original condition when Wright was designing some of his most famous structures.

Navy Pier

Built in 1916 and extending one mile out onto Lake Michigan, Navy Pier is Chicago's number one tourist attraction. Complete with a 150-foot-tall Ferris wheel, IMAX Theatre, musical carousel, Shakespeare Theater, Children's Museum, and boat cruises, this summer playground also hosts many festivals and fireworks.

Musical Carousel *(top)*

Designed exclusively for Navy Pier, this fanciful work-of-art delights children with its 36 hand-painted horses, chariots, and frog. Installed in 1995 and located near the Ferris wheel, the carousel recreates the golden age of the 1920's.

Ferris Wheel *(bottom)*

The world's first Ferris wheel was introduced in 1893 at the Columbian Exposition Fair in Chicago by George W. Ferris. Today, the Ferris wheel on Navy Pier is one of the pier's main attractions and offers extraordinary views of downtown Chicago and the lake.

Water Marks *(top)*

Located in Gateway Park, four mosaic covered benches twist along a terrazzo path representing the map of the I & M Canal. This project, from the Chicago Public Art Group and the Canal Corridor Association, is one of the country's largest community public artworks.

Gateway Park Fountain *(bottom)*

Gateway Park Fountain is a favorite place where kids can cool down in the summertime. This square, black granite fountain features 24 water spouts that create ever-changing displays. Designed by WET Design, it is a welcoming focal point of Navy Pier.

BIGart

With ever changing sculptures and statues along Gateway Park, visitors are treated to a free outdoor exhibit of art from BIGart at Navy Pier. Known for creating enormous sculptures, Nancy Rubins' 36-foot-tall *Monochrome II Chicago* is made from discarded aluminum canoes woven together with spider web-like cables.

Navy Pier

Officially named Navy Pier in 1927 to honor WWI Navy veterans, the pier was a hub of activity throughout the 1920's. During WWII, it was closed to the public and used to train an estimated 60,000 servicemen. Today, it attracts more than 8.6 million visitors a year.

Chicago Harbor Light

Originally situated at the mouth of the
Chicago River, the Chicago Harbor Light
was moved to its current location in 1919.
Equipped with a third-order Fresnel lens
from the World's Colombian Exposition,
today this lighthouse is owned and operated by the City of Chicago and designated a National Historic Landmark.

Lakefront Trail

The Lakefront Trail is one of the best ways to see the city. Connecting many of the city's points of interest, this 18-mile trail is used by Chicagoans for marathon training, biking, skating, and roller blading. Equipped with washrooms and drinking fountains, visitors enjoy breathtaking sunrise, sunset, and lake views.

Race at Mackinac

With over 100 years of honor, prestige, trophies, and bragging rights on the line, the "Mac" is one of the longest freshwater sailing races in the country. It attracts sailors from Europe, Asia, and Australia, as well as American sailors from Maine to California.

Sailboat Race at Mackinac *(top and bottom)*

The 333-mile-long race from the mouth of the Chicago River to Mackinac Island is a test of teamwork, endurance, and character. Bad weather and two world wars have not stopped sailors from trying to win the silver hardware and a place in history alongside names like Roy Disney and Steve Fossett.

Skyline *(pages 98 - 99)*

Out of the ashes of the Great Chicago Fire of 1871, Chicago has risen to be a cultural, dining, and architectural leader in the world. As the hub of commerce, labor, and trade at the turn of the 20th century, the city was built by proud immigrants and business leaders.

Summer Along the Lakeshore

Chicagoans really know how to make the most out of the more than 25 miles of lakefront. Operated by the City of Chicago, the lakefront beaches are free, clean, and most have life guards. Everything from dog beaches to outdoor dining is available along the lakeshore.

Lincoln Park Zoo

Lions and tigers and bears are just a few of the 1,250 animals housed at this historic zoo. A treasure since 1868, the zoo is free and open 365 days a year. Must see exhibits include Farm-in-the-Zoo, Regenstein African Journey, and Regenstein Center for African Apes.

Dream Lady

Located in the gardens of Lincoln Park Zoo, this monument was created in honor of children's poet Eugene Field. In 1922, Chicago public school children and private citizens donated money for this statue of an angel hovering over sleeping children. Two child-level drinking fountains are on either side of the base.

Oz Park *(above, right, and opposite)*

Inspired by the World's Columbian Exhibition, L. Frank Baum wrote the *Wonderful Wizard of Oz* while living in Chicago. In 1995, John Kearney began to sculpt its main characters. Located in Lincoln Park, children delight in seeing the larger-than-life Tin Man, Scarecrow, Cowardly Lion, Dorothy, and Toto.

Skyline *(above)*

Whether day or night, the Chicago skyline is breathtaking. From the Museum Campus peninsula, the full perspective of the city's architecture gleams in the sunshine. With white, black, copper, and glass structures in all shapes and sizes, the skyline is always fascinating.

The 'L' *(left)*

The elevated train system in Chicago is the lifeblood of the city and the gateway to Chicago's neighborhoods. Most landmarks, museums, and popular sights are accessible by one of eight main lines which are color-coded for easy navigation. Nicknamed the 'L,' it sees more than 700,000 riders each weekday.

George Washington, Robert Morris, Hyam Salomon Memorial

Dressed in his Revolutionary War uniform, George Washington shakes hands with two major financers of the war, Robert Morris and Haym Salomon. Designed by Lorado Taft and located on Wacker Drive, this sculpture honors their willingness to take financial risks for the Patriot cause.

Christopher Columbus (*opposite*)

Located next to Columbus Drive in Grant Park, this 1933 statue by Carlo Brioschi was paid for by Chicago's Italian-American community. Columbus is depicted surveying the horizon while holding a map in his right hand. Around the base are allegorical busts of Faith, Strength, Freedom, and Courage.

Abraham Lincoln, Head of State (*above*)

Augustus Saint-Gaudens' bronze statue in Grant Park features the 16th President in a massive chair draped with the president's shawl. The figure's face and hands were created from actual casts of Lincoln and evokes a sense of loneliness Lincoln felt during the Civil War.

Vietnam Veterans Memorial Plaza

Located on the Riverwalk, Chicago's Vietnam memorial is one of the largest Vietnam memorials outside of Washington, D.C. Dedicated in 2005, it features a wall listing the more than 2,900 Illinois veterans who served their country during the war; a reflecting pool; and a waterfall with a sculpture of the Vietnam service medal.

Ulysses S. Grant Memorial

Sitting astride Cincinnati, the horse General Grant rode into battle during the Civil War, this monument was created in 1891 to memorialize the general. Standing 18 feet high, artist Louis Rebisso created a Romanesque arched structure that conveyed the strength and honor of this commander and two-term president.

Fireworks

Chicagoans love fireworks and Navy Pier
is the place to view a spectacular show.
Synchronized to music, summer fireworks
can be viewed from a charter boat on the
lake or from pier-side.

Festival of Lights

Each year Chicago is dressed up for winter and the holiday season with hundreds of thousands of lights in the trees all along Michigan Avenue. The North Michigan Avenue Society inaugurates the festivities with a spectacular parade that features fireworks and special guest - Mickey Mouse.

Chicago Pow Wow Festival *(above and left)*

Hosted by the American Indian Center of Chicago at Navy Pier, this colorful festival is over 60 years old. With exhibitions of ritual dances and traditional ceremonies, authentic Native American food, and special gifts handmade in time-honored ways, kids and families come from all over to enjoy the festivities.

Kawansila Totem Pole *(opposite)*

Carved by Tony Hunt, the hereditary chief of the Kwagu'ł Tribe, this pole replaces the original one that was donated in 1929 by James L. Kraft. Located in Lincoln Park, it stands 40 feet tall. Carved into the pole is a sea monster, a whale, and Kwanusila, the Thunderbird.

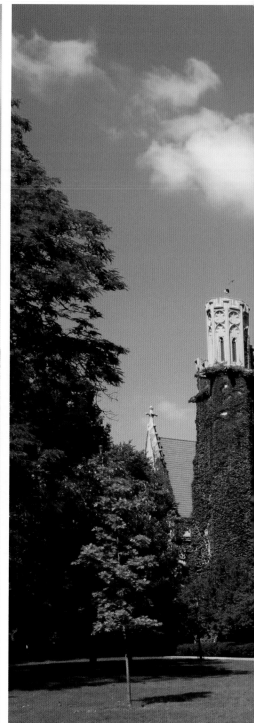

The Bowman

The Spearman and *The Bowman* were erected in 1928 on either side of the entrance to Grant Park at Congress Parkway and Michigan Avenue. *The Bowman,* pictured here, represents a Native American with archer posture and muscles in tension. Croatian sculpture Ivan Meštrović intentionally did not give the warriors weapons.

University of Chicago

With land donated in Hyde Park by Marshall Field and money donated by John D. Rockefeller, the University was founded in 1890 on the principle of bringing a community of great scholars together to better the world. Most buildings on the campus were created in the English Gothic style of architecture.

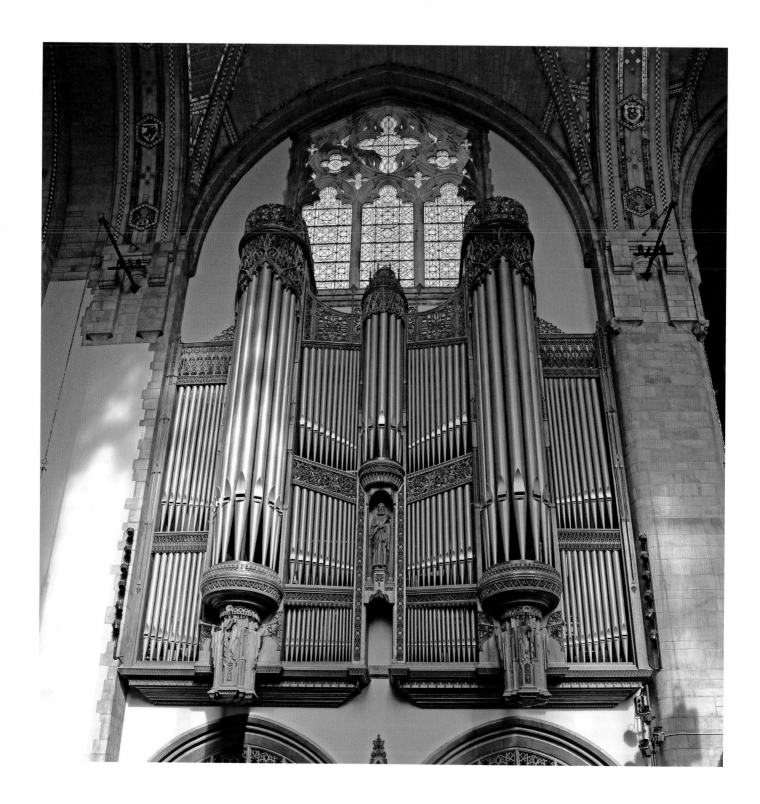

E.M. Skinner Organ

The E.M. Skinner Organ was built in 1928 when the chapel was built for John D. Rockefeller. The Opus 634 was created to emulate the sounds of a symphony orchestra, including choral voices. After complete restoration in 2008, the organ now has 8,565 pipes in 132 ranks.

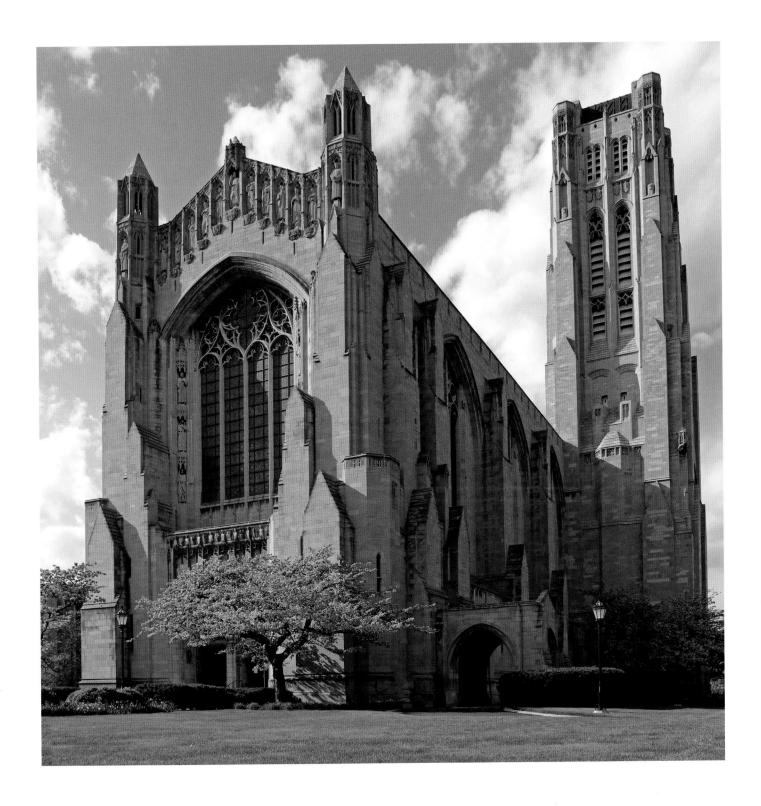

Rockefeller Memorial Chapel

Built to be the tallest structure on campus, Rockefeller Memorial Chapel has over 100 stone sculptures, a 25-foot chancel window, and its Carillon with 72 bells is the single largest musical instrument ever built. This non-denominational chapel also has an outdoor pulpit for open air services.

GREAT PYRAMID
GIZA EGYPT
2600 B.C.

WORLD TRADE CENTER—2001
NEW YORK

THE ALAMO TEXAS

Tribune Tower *(above, left, and opposite)*

Built to be the most beautiful office building in the world, this 1925 neo-Gothic tower is complete with buttresses, spires, and grotesques. Before its completion, Tribune owner Colonel McCormick requested correspondents to bring rocks and bricks back from around the world. More than 135 fragments are incorporated in the building's wall.

United Center *(top)*

Home to the Chicago Bulls and Blackhawks, the United Center is both a sports and entertainment venue. Hosting more than 200 events a year and with a seating capacity of 23,500, it has been nicknamed, "The house that Michael Jordan built."

Soldier Field *(bottom)*

This state-of-the-art stadium was renovated in 2003 and seats 61,500. The original Soldier Field, named in memory of American soldiers lost in battle, was the site of the first Special Olympic Games. Today, it is home to the city's beloved Chicago Bears.

The Spirit *(opposite)*

"The best there ever was. The best there ever will be." These words are inscribed in the base of *The Spirit*, the 12-foot-tall statue of basketball legend, Michael Jordan. Unveiled on the same day Jordan's number was retired, it is one of Chicago's favorite attractions.

MICHAEL JORDAN

CHICAGO BULLS

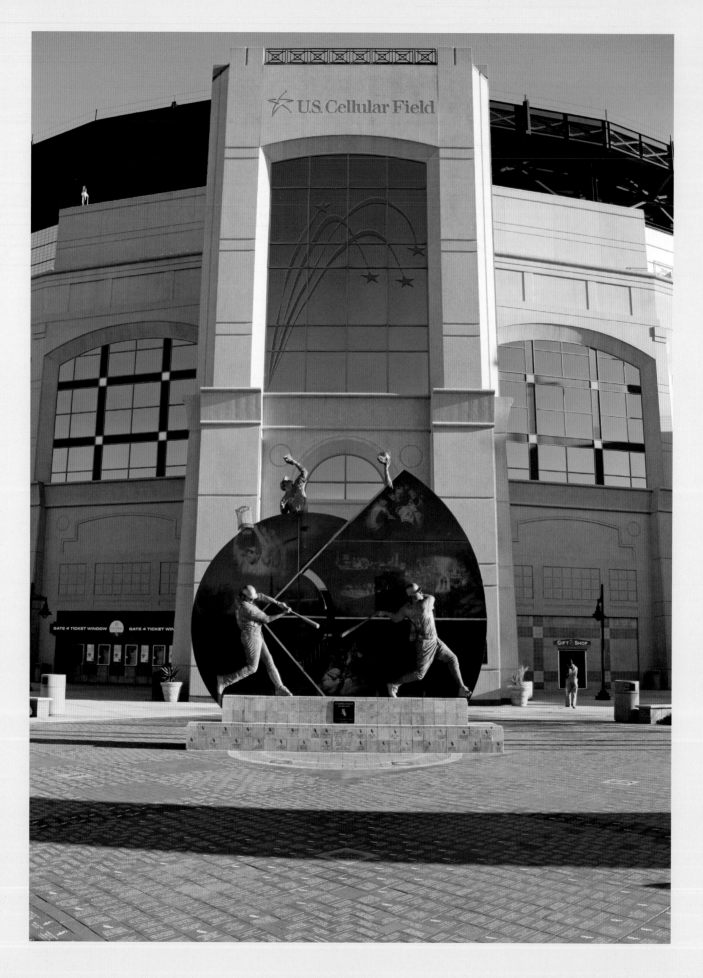

Wrigley Field *(above)*

The Northside field located in Wrigleyville has been home to the Chicago Cubs since 1916. Famous for its ivy covered outfield walls and hand-turned score board, this is the second oldest baseball field in the United States. Neighborhood rooftops around Wrigley Field are another popular way to watch the games.

Harry Caray *(right)*

Beloved voice of the Chicago Cubs, Harry Caray was a broadcast legend in baseball. Best known for his 7th-inning rendition of "Take Me Out to the Ball Game," this memorial is located outside Wrigley Field.

U.S. Cellular Field *(opposite)*

U.S. Cellular Field opened in 1991 and is home to the Chicago White Sox. Originally named the White Stockings, the team has been a Southside fixture since 1901. Special features of the park include a replica of Comiskey Park's exploding scoreboard, the FUNdamentals skills deck, and the Rain Room.

Chicago Air and Water Show

For two days along the Chicago lakefront, more than 2 million spectators look to the sky and watch as planes whirl and twirl through death-defying feats. Beginning in 1959 as the Lakeshore Park Air & Water Show, this show has since evolved into a popular summertime festival.

Thunderbirds

Visible by boat or beach, this free event includes favorites such as the Thunderbirds, Blue Angels, Golden Nights, Navy Leap Frogs, and the Chicago Fire Department Air and Sea Rescue Team. Vistors that arrive a day early can watch the Friday practice show and avoid the crowds.

Tom Barrat

Tom is a Chicago-based photographer specializing in travel, wild-life, and architecture. With a portfolio of digital images from all over the United States and 25 countries, he is a contributing stock photographer to a number of internet sites, as well as to his own website. During the last four years, he has had over 25,000 images downloaded for use on websites, annual reports, newspapers, magazine ads, books, and other print media, with more than half being used internationally. He is a former executive in software development, internet banking, and debit card processing. Visit TomBarratPhotography.com to learn more about him.

Courtney Pitt

Courtney Pitt was born and raised in Chicagoland. After attending Boston University for journalism, she moved back to Chicago to work in the magazine industry, writing and editing for both *Chicago* magazine and *Chicago-Scene Magazine*. Courtney is now the President of a strategic marketing and business development firm. She also devotes her free time to philanthropic efforts that help the people and the city she loves. Courtney lives on the north side of Chicago with her supportive husband and two wonderful daughters. To learn more about Courtney, visit CourtneyPitt.com.